# Literature Circle Guide:

# From the Mixed-up Files of Mrs. Basil E. Frankweiler

by Perdita Finn

SCHOLASTIC
PROFESSIONAL BOOKS

**New York • Toronto • London • Auckland • Sydney**
**• Mexico City • New Delhi • Hong Kong • Buenos Aires**

Guide written by Perdita Finn
Edited by Sarah Glasscock
Cover design by Niloufar Safavieh
Interior design by Grafica, Inc.
Interior illustrations by Mona Mark

Credits:
(Cover) FROM THE MIXED-UP FILES OF MRS. BASIL E. FRANKWEILER by E. L. Konigsburg. Cover art copyright © 1967 by E.L. Konigsburg. Used by permission of Random House Children's Books, a division of Random House, Inc.
(Interior) Author photo on page 9 courtesy of Simon & Schuster, NY.

ISBN 0-439-16360-9

Printed in the U.S.A.

# Contents

# To the Teacher

As a teacher, you naturally want to instill in your students the habits of confident, critical, independent, and lifelong readers. You hope that even when students are not in school they will seek out books on their own, think about and question what they are reading, and share those ideas with friends. An excellent way to further this goal is by using literature circles in your classroom.

In a literature circle, students select a book to read as a group. They think and write about it on their own in a literature response journal and then discuss it together. Both journals and discussions enable students to respond to a book and develop their insights into it. They also learn to identify themes and issues, analyze vocabulary, recognize writing techniques, and share ideas with each other—all of which are necessary to meet state and national standards.

This guide provides the support materials for using literature circles with *The Mixed-up Files of Mrs. Basil E. Frankweiler* by E.L. Konigsburg. The reading strategies, discussion questions, projects, and enrichment readings will also support a whole class reading of this text or can be given to enhance the experience of an individual student reading the book as part of a reading workshop.

## Literature Circles

A literature circle consists of several students (usually three to five) who agree to read a book together and share their observations, questions, and interpretations. Groups may be organized by reading level or choice of book. Often these groups read more than one book together since, as students become more comfortable talking with one another, their observations and insights deepen.

When planning to use literature circles in your classroom, it can be helpful to do the following:

✻ Recommend four or five books from which students can choose. These books might be grouped by theme, genre, or author.

✻ Allow three or four weeks for students to read each book. Each of Scholastic's *Literature Circle Guides* has the same number of sections as well as enrichment activities and final projects. Even if students are reading different books in the *Literature Circle Guide* series, they can be scheduled to finish at the same time.

✻ Create a daily routine so students can focus on journal writing and discussions.

✻ Decide whether students will be reading books in class or for homework. If students do all their reading for homework, then allot class time for sharing journals and discussions. You can also alternate silent reading and writing days in the classroom with discussion groups.

> ### Read More About Literature Circles
>
> *Getting the Most from Literature Groups* by Penny Strube (Scholastic Professional Books, 1996)
>
> *Literature Circles* by Harvey Daniels (Stenhouse Publishers, 1994)

# Using the *Literature Circle Guides* in Your Classroom

Each guide contains the following sections:

* background information about the author and book
* enrichment readings relevant to the book
* Literature Response Journal reproducibles
* Group Discussion reproducibles
* Individual and group projects
* Literature Discussion Evaluation Sheet

## Background Information and Enrichment Readings

The background information about the author and the book and the enrichment readings are designed to offer information that will enhance students' understanding of the book. You may choose to assign and discuss these sections before, during, or after the reading of the book. Because each enrichment concludes with questions that invite students to connect it to the book, you can use this section to inspire students to think and record their thoughts in the literature response journal.

## Literature Response Journal Reproducibles

Although these reproducibles are designed for individual students, they should also be used to stimulate and support discussions in literature circles. Each page begins with a reading strategy and follows with several journal topics. At the bottom of the page, students select a type of response (prediction, question, observation, or connection) for free-choice writing in their response journals.

### ◆ Reading Strategies
Since the goal of the literature circle is to empower lifelong readers, a different reading strategy is introduced in each section. Not only does the reading strategy allow students to understand this particular book better, it also instills a habit of mind that will continue to be useful when they read other books. A question from the Literature Response Journal and the Group Discussion pages is always tied to the reading strategy.

If everyone in class is reading the same book, you may present the reading strategy as a mini-lesson to the entire class. For literature circles, however, the group of students can read over and discuss the strategy together at the start of class and then experiment with the strategy as they read silently for the rest of the period. You may want to allow time at the end of class so the group can talk about what they noticed as they read. As an alternative, the literature circle can review the reading strategy for the next section after they have completed their discussion. That night, students can try out the reading strategy as they read on their own so they will be ready for the next day's literature circle discussion.

### ◆ Literature Response Journal Topics
A literature response journal allows a reader to "converse" with a book. Students write questions, point out things they notice about the story, recall personal experiences, and make connections to other texts in their journals. In other words, they are using writing to explore what they think about the book. See page 7 for tips on how to help students set up their literature response journals.

**1.** The questions for the literature response journals have no right or wrong answers but are designed to help students look beneath the surface of the plot and develop a richer connection to the story and its characters.

**2.** Students can write in their literature response journals as soon as they have finished a reading assignment. Again, you may choose to have students do this for homework or make time during class.

**3.** The literature response journals are an excellent tool for students to use in their literature circles. They can highlight ideas and thoughts in their journals that they want to share with the group.

**4.** When you evaluate students' journals, consider whether they have completed all the assignments and have responded in depth and thoughtfully. You may want to check each day to make sure students are keeping up with the assignments. You can read and respond to the journals at a halfway point (after five entries) and again at the end. Some teachers suggest that students pick out their five best entries for a grade.

## Group Discussion Reproducibles

These reproducibles are designed for use in literature circles. Each page begins with a series of discussion questions for the group to consider. A mini-lesson on an aspect of the writer's craft follows the discussion questions. See page 8 for tips on how to model good discussions for students.

◆ **Literature Discussion Questions:** In a literature discussion, students experience a book from different points of view. Each reader brings her or his own unique observations, questions, and associations to the text. When students share their different reading experiences, they often come to a wider and deeper understanding than they would have reached on their own.

The discussion is not an exercise in finding the right answers nor is it a debate. Its goal is to explore the many possible meanings of a book. Be sure to allow enough time for these conversations to move beyond easy answers—try to schedule 25–35 minutes for each one. In addition, there are important guidelines to ensure that everyone's voice is heard.

**1.** Let students know that participation in the literature discussion is an important part of their grade. You may choose to watch one discussion and grade it. (You can use the Literature Discussion Evaluation Sheet on page 33.)

**2.** Encourage students to evaluate their own performance in discussions using the Literature Discussion Evaluation Sheet. They can assess not only their own level of involvement but also how the group itself has functioned.

**3.** Help students learn how to talk to one another effectively. After a discussion, help them process what worked and what didn't. Videotape discussions if possible, and then evaluate them together. Let one literature circle watch another and provide feedback to it.

**4.** It can be helpful to have a facilitator for each discussion. The facilitator can keep students from interrupting each other, help the conversation get back on track when it digresses, and encourage shyer members to contribute. At the end of each discussion, the facilitator can summarize everyone's contributions and suggest areas for improvement.

**5.** Designate other roles for group members. For instance, a recorder can take notes and/or list questions for further discussion. A summarizer can open each literature circle meeting by summarizing the chapter(s) the group has just read. Encourage students to rotate these roles, as well as that of the facilitator.

◆ **The Writer's Craft:** This section encourages students to look at the writer's most important tool—words. It points out new vocabulary, writing techniques, and uses of language. One or two questions invite students to think more deeply about the book and writing in general. These questions can either become part of the literature circle discussion or be written about in students' journals.

## Literature Discussion Evaluation Sheet

Both you and your students will benefit from completing these evaluation sheets. You can use them to assess students' performance, and as mentioned above, students can evaluate their own individual performances, as well as their group's performance. The Literature Discussion Evaluation Sheet appears on page 33.

# Setting Up Literature Response Journals

Although some students may already keep literature response journals, others may not know how to begin. To discourage students from merely writing elaborate plot summaries and to encourage them to use their journals in a meaningful way, help them focus their responses around the following elements: predictions, observations, questions, and connections.

Have students take time after each assigned section to think about and record their responses in their journals. Sample responses appear below.

◆ **Predictions:** Before students read the book, have them take the time to study the cover and the jacket copy. Ask if anyone has read any other books by E.L. Konigsburg. To begin their literature response journals, tell students to jot down their impressions about the book. As they read, students will continue to make predictions about what a character might do or how the plot might turn. After finishing the book, students can re-assess their initial predictions. Good readers understand that they must constantly activate prior knowledge before, during, and after they read. They adjust their expectations and predictions; a book that is completely predictable is not likely to capture anyone's interest. A student about to read *The Mixed-up Files of Mrs. Basil E. Frankweiler* for the first time might predict the following:

> *This might be kind of a mystery story. I bet that Claudia, Jamie, and Mrs. Frankweiler team up to solve the mystery of who made the statue. I bet that Mrs. Frankweiler is rich, too—and maybe lonely.*

◆ **Observations:** This activity takes place immediately after reading begins. In a literature response journal, the reader recalls fresh impressions about the characters, setting, and events. Most readers mention details that stand out for them even if they are not sure what their importance is. For example, a reader might list phrases that describe how a character looks or the feeling a setting evokes. Many readers note certain words, phrases, or passages in a book.

Others note the style of an author's writing or the voice in which the story is told. A student just starting to read *The Mixed-up Files of Mrs. Basil E. Frankweiler* might write the following:

> *I think I know more about how Claudia is going to run away than why! She seems to think of everything—I would never be that organized. It sounds like she lives somewhere close to New York City. She doesn't talk about her parents very much—she doesn't even seem that mad at them. It's not like they had a big fight or anything.*

◆ **Questions:** Point out that good readers don't necessarily understand everything they read. To clarify their uncertainty, they ask questions. Encourage students to identify passages that confuse or trouble them, and emphasize that they shouldn't take anything for granted. Share the following student example:

> *Why is Claudia running away? Isn't she worried about how upsetting it's going to be for her mom and dad? How come she's not scared to go to New York City? And who is Mrs. Basil E. Frankweiler, and what does she have to do with the story?*

◆ **Connections:** Remind students that one story often leads to another. When one friend tells a story, another friend is often inspired to tell one, too. The same thing often happens when someone reads a book. A character reminds the reader of a relative, or a situation is similar to something that happened to him or her. Sometimes a book makes a reader recall other books or movies. These connections can be helpful in revealing some of the deeper meanings or patterns of a book. The following is an example of a student connection:

> *Claudia reminds me a lot of myself—she sounds like a really good student, and I get good grades, too. She likes hot-fudge sundaes, just like I do. Only I don't think I'd ever have the courage to run away, even if I wanted to.*

# The Good Discussion

In a good literature discussion, students are always learning from one another. They listen to one another and respond to what their peers have to say. They share their ideas, questions, and observations. Everyone feels comfortable about talking, and no one interrupts or puts down what anyone else says. Students leave a good literature discussion with a new understanding of the book—and sometimes with new questions about it. They almost always feel more engaged by what they have read.

◆ **Modeling a Good Discussion:** In this era of combative and confessional TV talk shows, students often don't have any idea of what it means to talk productively and creatively together. You can help them have a better idea of what a good literature discussion is if you let them experience one. Select a thought-provoking short story or poem for students to read, and then choose a small group to model a discussion of the work for the class.

Explain to participating students that the objective of the discussion is to explore the text thoroughly and learn from one another. Emphasize that it takes time to learn how to have a good discussion, and that the first discussion may not achieve everything they hope it will. Duplicate a copy of the Literature Discussion Evaluation Sheet for each student. Go over the helpful and unhelpful contributions shown on the Literature Discussion Evaluation Sheet. Instruct students to fill it out as they watch the model discussion. Then have the group of students hold its discussion while the rest of the class observes. Try not to interrupt or control the discussion and remind the student audience not to participate. It's okay if the discussion falters, as this is a learning experience

Allow 15–20 minutes for the discussion. When it is finished, ask each student in the group to reflect out loud about what worked and what didn't. Then have the students who observed share their impressions. What kinds of comments were helpful? How could the group have talked to each other more productively? You may want to let another group experiment with a discussion so students can try out what they learned from the first one.

◆ **Assessing Discussions:** The following tips will help students monitor how well their group is functioning:

**1.** One person should keep track of all behaviors by each group member, both helpful and unhelpful, during the discussion.

**2.** At the end of the discussion, each individual should think about how he or she did. How many helpful and unhelpful checks did he or she receive?

**3.** The group should look at the Literature Discussion Evaluation Sheet and assess their performance as a whole. Were most of the behaviors helpful? Were any behaviors unhelpful? How could the group improve?

---

In good discussions, you will often hear students say the following:

*"I was wondering if anyone knew . . ."*

*"I see what you are saying. That reminds me of something that happened earlier in the book."*

*"What do you think?"*

*"Did anyone notice on page 57 that . . ."*

*"I disagree with you because . . ."*

*"I agree with you because . . ."*

*"This reminds me so much of when . . ."*

*"Do you think this could mean . . ."*

*"I'm not sure I understand what you're saying. Could you explain it a little more to me?"*

*"That reminds me of what you were saying yesterday about . . ."*

*"I just don't understand this."*

*"I love the part that says . . ."*

*"Here, let me read this paragraph. It's an example of what I'm talking about."*

## About *From the Mixed-up Files of Mrs. Basil E. Frankweiler*

When *From the Mixed-up Files of Mrs. Basil E. Frankweiler* was first published over thirty years ago, it was an immediate success. The book won many awards, including the Newbery Medal in 1968. Critics went wild, calling it "fast and fresh and funny," and "one of the most original stories of many years." Most of all, kids everywhere fell in love with it—with the realistic characters, their crazy adventures, humor, and secrets. E.L. Konigsburg's daughter, Laurie, has said that her mother's success can be attributed to the fact that "when children read any of her novels, they see themselves, and they laugh."

## About the Author: E.L. Konigsburg

E.L. Konigsburg was inspired to write *From the Mixed-up Files of Mrs. Basil E. Frankweiler* while listening to her three children Laurie, Paul, and Ross complain about the insects and heat during a family picnic. She realized that her kids, raised in the ease of the suburbs, would never feel driven to run away to have a wilderness adventure like Huck Finn and Tom Sawyer, but would instead want to hide in some place splendid and comfortable—like the Metropolitan Museum of Art in New York City. Like many writers, Konigsburg looked at the ordinary happenings in her life and asked, "What if?"

Elaine Lobl Konigsburg began writing when her youngest child started school. Her first book *Jennifer, Hecate, Macbeth, William McKinley, and Me, Elizabeth* was based on her daughter's experiences adjusting to a new school and making friends. A later novel, *About the B'nai Bagels*, came from her son's involvement in Little League, football, and basketball. When Konigsburg did the illustrations for those early books, she even had her own children model for her.

The author also put much of herself into her characters as well. According to her daughter, she has an organizational system a lot like Mrs. Frankweiler's. Her husband reports that E.L. Konigsburg is a sharp poker player, just like Jamie, and she went through school with straight A's, just like Claudia.

E.L. Konigsburg loved to read books when she was little, often hiding in the bathroom to do so, but she never thought she would be a writer. She went to the Carnegie Institute of Technology and studied chemistry. As Konigsburg's husband says, "After a few minor explosions, burned hair, and stained and torn clothes, she began to think about other occupations." For a while she taught science, then she studied art seriously in New York City, and finally embarked on a career as a writer.

E.L. Konigsburg has said that, in writing her books, she is always interested in how people discover who they are. She admits that even as a grandmother she is still working out who she is. "I have changed as a result of each book I've written. When I have finished a book, I am no longer the person who started it and part of the reason is because I wrote that book."

# Enrichment: Michelangelo

Have you ever tried to make a sculpture with modeling clay? If so, you know just how hard it is to capture the exact proportions and lines of a face or a hand. Imagine just how much harder it would be if you were working with hard marble, slowly chipping at it with a hammer and a chisel. That is what Michelangelo most loved to do—take a piece of rock and transform it so that it actually looked like a living, breathing body.

Michelangelo Buonarroti was born in Tuscany, Italy, on March 6, 1475. His mother was too sick to care for him, and as a baby, he was sent to live with a family of stonecutters. There Michelangelo fell in love with the craft of sculpture. When he told his father what he wanted to do, his father was furious. "Artists are laborers, no better than shoemakers," he said. Eventually, however, his father gave in and sent Michelangelo at age 13 to study with the successful painter Ghirlandaio.

One of the things Michelangelo studied was human anatomy. At the time, this was generally forbidden, and he had to get special permission from the Church to look at dead bodies so he could understand how the muscles and bones and veins beneath the skin really worked. Michelangelo also studied classical statues from Ancient Rome, which at the time had recently been rediscovered and dug up.

At the age of 25, Michelangelo created what many people think is the greatest sculpture ever made—the *Madonna della Pietà*. It shows Mary, the mother of Jesus, holding the dead Christ across her lap. Giorgio Vasari, a writer of the time, wrote, "It is certainly a miracle that a formless block of stone could ever have been reduced to a perfection that nature is scarcely able to create in the flesh."

Just days after this Pietà was placed in Saint Peter's Basilica in Rome (where it still is today), Michelangelo overheard someone remark that the work was done by a different artist. In a fit of rage, he carved the following inscription on the sash running across Mary's breast: MICHEL ANGELUS BONAROTUS FLORENT FACIBAT (*Michelangelo Buonarroti, Florentine, made this*). This is the only piece Michelangelo ever signed. Later, he was embarrassed by his outburst of pride and decided never again to put his name on any of his creations.

Michelangelo went on to produce many more famous sculptures—*David, Moses,* the *Dying Slave,* and more Pietàs. He became a famous painter, even working upside down for many years, covering the Sistine Chapel's ceiling with images from the Bible. He was an architect as well and designed not only the beautiful Medici library in Florence but also St. Peter's Basilica, the model for the Capitol in Washington, D.C.

Always, however, Michelangelo returned to sculpture. Often he would stay up all night chiseling rock. He even made a cardboard helmet upon which he fixed a candle to light his work and keep his hands free. Many of these later statues remained unfinished. Michelangelo destroyed some statues because they weren't as good as he wanted them to be.

On a cold, rainy day in February 1564, Michelangelo went riding in the countryside. When he returned home, he was ill. He died six days later.

As you read *From The Mixed-up Files of Mrs. Basil E. Frankweiler*, you may find yourself wanting to know more about the life of Michelangelo. Like Claudia and Jamie, you can visit a library (or surf the 'Net) and find out many more colorful details about his long, rich life. If you want to discover something about Michelangelo's genius as a sculptor, however, you may want to invite your art teacher or a local artist to come and work with you on some sculpture. There's no better way to learn to appreciate someone else's art than to create your own.

# Enrichment: Art Mysteries

One day a man drove up to Christie's, a famous auction house in New York City, with a painting strapped to the roof of his car. He claimed it was a famous Renaissance masterpiece by Dosso Dossi. The painting was beautiful but torn and dirty. How could the auctioneers tell whether it was worth millions of dollars or less than a box of crayons?

When an unknown painting or sculpture turns up, figuring out when it was painted or sculpted and who created it can take a lot of work. Usually the museum or the auction house will bring together a group of people who are experts on the period of time when the art was created and on the artist who made the piece. What they do first is look. Does it look like other paintings and sculptures from the same time period? Does it look like other Michelangelo's or other Dossi's? Are the colors, subject matter, brush strokes, or chisel marks recognizable? When Jamie sits in the Donnell library studying sculptures made by Michelangelo, he is beginning to familiarize himself with the artist's style.

It is, of course, possible to imitate someone else's style. Down through the centuries there have been master forgers who are skilled at creating works that look just like famous Rembrandts or Van Goghs. Even today some museums aren't entirely sure that all their art is authentic. Sometimes a plaque next to a painting will read "Attributed to. . ." instead of "By . . ." This means that the museum isn't absolutely sure who the artist is.

Recent advances in technology such as x-rays, carbon 14 dating, and chemical tests make it possible to test the materials used in paintings to see if they are what the actual artists would have used. Is the paper the same kind that was used in fourteenth-century Italy? Does the marble come from the particular rock quarry where Michelangelo bought his stone? Being able to answer such questions makes it much easier to determine when a work of art was created.

Yet even these tests can't reveal if the painting or sculpture was forged during the artist's lifetime by someone with access to all the same materials and even the advice of the artist himself. In Italy during the Renaissance, a successful sculptor or painter would have had many apprentices and students trying to imitate his style.

Because of this, one of the most important pieces of evidence needed for solving an art mystery is proof that the artist in question actually created a particular piece. Such proof could be a sketch for that particular work of art in one of the artist's notebooks, a passage in a friend's diary describing him working on it, or even a receipt from the first person who bought it.

Recently in England, an art forger was caught who was not only imitating the styles of famous early twentieth-century painters, but also forging proof of the paintings' authenticity. The mastermind behind the forgeries, John Drewe, was sneaking into art libraries and carefully changing letters, accounts, and gallery catalogues to make it seem that his forgeries were real. Apparently, the forgeries themselves (painted by a high school art teacher down on his luck) weren't very good, and the materials he used were not even appropriate. The documentation, however, was so convincing that everyone believed that these were the works of famous painters.

The question that came up during Drewe's trial was whether or not it matters who created a painting or sculpture. After it was authenticated, the Dossi painting sold for millions of dollars to the Getty Museum. Was that its true value? Does it matter if the angel sculpture is by Michelangelo or not? Is it any less beautiful? Is it worth any less? Michelangelo himself spent years copying famous classical sculptures, trying as hard as he could to make them look like they were from Ancient Rome. Those copies today are now priceless.

# Enrichment: Museums

The first true museum, the Great Library at Alexandria, was created more than two thousand years ago, in 290 B.C., by Ptolemy I Soter of Egypt. A place for scholars to study and learn, it included a dining hall, a botanical garden with both rare and local plants, a zoo, and an astronomical observatory. There was also a collection of surgical instruments, animal hides, statues, and portraits that were used in teaching. Above all, it had the greatest collection of books in the Ancient World—more than half a million volumes or papyrus rolls.

In many ways, the Great Library at Alexandria wasn't that different from the museums we visit today with their science or history or art collections, libraries, and cafeterias. Certainly their goals are the same—to collect and preserve important objects and use them to educate people.

*Museum* is a Latin word that comes from the Greek *mouseion,* meaning a temple dedicated to the nine Muses—goddesses of the arts and learning. The ancient Greek temples were filled with statues, vases, paintings, and ornaments dedicated to the gods, and displayed for the public to see and learn from. During the Middle Ages in Europe, churches were like museums, housing collections of religious art and statues, manuscripts, and saints' relics.

These early museums also housed booty captured in wars from foreign places. The Roman Army brought back all kinds of strange new animals, plants, and objects from the lands it occupied. The Crusaders likewise brought back what they had plundered and stolen from the Holy Lands. Many museum collections today are the result of the occupation of foreign countries, and the ownership of these works of art has come into question. Recently, Greece asked England to return the famous Elgin Marbles, and different Native American communities have requested that their sacred objects no longer be displayed.

Most of the objects you see at a modern museum, however, were either donated by

wealthy benefactors or bought directly by the museum itself. An art collector like Mrs. Frankweiler would be courted by a museum in hopes that she might donate a valuable piece.

Today there are over 24,000 significant museums all over the world. One of the very biggest is the Metropolitan Museum of Art in New York City. It was founded in 1870 by a group of Americans—businessmen as well as leading artists and thinkers—to bring art and art education to the American people. It has painting, sculpture, furniture, costume, and jewelry collections from all over the world and different periods of time, from ancient Egypt to the twentieth century. It also has numerous educational programs, a conservation section that restores and researches objects and paintings, and the largest art and archaeology reference library in the world.

When you visit a museum, one thing to think about is why the museum has chosen to display the objects, paintings, and/or sculptures it does. What do the people who run the museum want to show us and teach us? Why would the Metropolitan Museum of Art, for instance, purchase a work like the angel sculpture in this story? Why do you think the museum would want to have the piece in its collection? Why would the museum want people to have a chance to see this particular sculpture?

Name _____     Date _____

## *From the Mixed-up Files of Mrs. Basil E. Frankweiler*
## Before Reading the Book

## Reading Strategy: Having Expectations About a Book

*From the Mixed-up Files of Mrs. Basil E. Frankweiler* is a famous book. Even though you haven't read it, you may already have heard about it from your teacher, your parents (who may have loved it when they were kids!), or your friends. What have you heard? How does that make you feel about reading the book? What do you imagine reading the book will be like? What do you imagine will happen in it? It's important to know that some of your expectations will be met and others will not.

## Writing in Your Literature Response Journal

**A.** Write about one of these topics in your journal. Circle the topic you chose.

**1.** Consider the title of this book. What does it make you think about and why? Based upon the title, what are your expectations about the book?

**2.** Describe as carefully as you can a painting, a photograph, or a piece of sculpture that has captured your attention. You may have fallen in love with it or you may not like it at all, but for some reason you can't stop thinking about it. Where did you first see it? What were your first thoughts about it? What were your questions? What do you think about it now?

**3.** Imagine you have been chosen to join a team of explorers. What special skills, abilities, or interests do you have that made them decide to take you? Write about some of the exceptional things you have done or are good at. Do any of your skills or abilities ever get you in trouble? Perhaps, for instance, you are good at asking questions. How could that be both an asset and a problem?

**B.** What were your predictions, questions, observations, and connections about the book? Write about one of them in your journal. Check the response you chose.

❑ Prediction     ❑ Question     ❑ Observation     ❑ Connection

Literature Circle Guide for *From the Mixed-up Files of Mrs. Basil E. Frankweiler* • Scholastic Professional Books

Name _____ Date _____

### *From the Mixed-up Files of Mrs. Basil E. Frankweiler*
## Before Reading the Book

## For Your Discussion Group

✳ If you have ever visited a museum, share your experiences. What did you see? What did you think about what you saw? If you could have done anything you wanted in the museum—even roller-bladed down the hallways—what would it have been?

✳ Now, as a group, take a real or virtual trip to an art museum. If you can't actually take a field trip, go online and visit the collections of some of the most famous museums in the world. You can also go to the library and look at art books, such as books on Renaissance painting and sculpture, Impressionism, or the paintings of Goya. Let yourself wander and browse just like you would through the galleries of a real museum.

✳ Members of your group may look at art in different ways, such as the following:

**Researcher**—You look at every picture in a room, book, or Web page and read all the information about the artist. Details interest you.

**Hit-and-run champ**—You look for a moment at this painting, then go across the room (or to the next page or book) to check out another, then down the hall (or onto another Web site) to an earlier period, and then back to where you started.

**Dreamer**—You stare at one painting for hours, wondering about it.

You may want to try all three ways of looking at art until you find one, or a combination, that feels natural. Remember that no one way is right.

✳ After your museum visit, talk about what you saw and what caught your attention. Was there a painting or sculpture you loved or hated? Tell what you noticed about the piece, what questions it made you ask, and what you imagined about it. Share with the group what you discovered about your personal viewing style.

Literature Circle Guide for *From the Mixed-up Files of Mrs. Basil E. Frankweiler* Scholastic Professional Books

Name _____ Date _____

*From the Mixed-up Files
of Mrs. Basil E. Frankweiler*
# Chapter 1

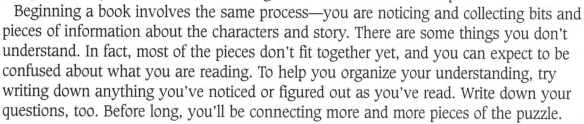

## Reading Strategy: Collecting Information

Before putting a jigsaw puzzle together, you must first
turn over the pieces and study them. For the moment,
you accept that you don't know what the big picture
looks like and you try to recognize what you can. Here
is a piece of sky; this is a corner of the girl's dress; here is a corner piece.

   Beginning a book involves the same process—you are noticing and collecting bits and
pieces of information about the characters and story. There are some things you don't
understand. In fact, most of the pieces don't fit together yet, and you can expect to be
confused about what you are reading. To help you organize your understanding, try
writing down anything you've noticed or figured out as you've read. Write down your
questions, too. Before long, you'll be connecting more and more pieces of the puzzle.

## Writing in Your Literature Response Journal

**A. Write about one of these topics in your journal. Circle the topic you chose.**

  **1.** This book begins with a **prologue**, a piece of writing before the first chapter. In
     this case, it is a letter from Mrs. Basil E. Frankweiler to her lawyer. What obvious
     and not-so-obvious things do you notice about this letter? What does it tell you
     about the story you are beginning to read?

  **2.** Claudia is running away. What prompted this action? What kind of person is she?
     Does Claudia remind you of anyone you know? If so, how does she resemble this
     person? What do you think about Claudia's plans?

**B. What were your predictions, questions, observations, and connections as you
read? Write about one of them in your journal. Check the response you chose.**

    ❏ Prediction    ❏ Question    ❏ Observation    ❏ Connection

Literature Circle Guide for *From the Mixed-up Files of Mrs. Basil E. Frankweiler* • Scholastic Professional Books

Name _____ Date _____

## *From the Mixed-up Files of Mrs. Basil E. Frankweiler*
## Chapter 1

### For Your Discussion Group

✳ In this first chapter, E.L. Konigsburg introduces three very interesting people—Claudia, Jamie, and Mrs. Frankweiler herself. On the one hand, Konigsburg explains a great deal about these characters—Claudia is "cautious" and Jamie is "adventurous"—but much of what we learn about them comes from watching how they behave and talk. For instance, what kind of person would run away to the Metropolitan Museum of Art? As readers, we can use these details as clues to interpret who these characters are.

✳ As a group, choose one of the characters to discuss. Then have each member of the group recall a specific action of that character from the first chapter. Talk together about what each action suggests about the character. Different group members may have different interpretations of the same actions.

✳ On pages 13–17, Claudia has a long conversation with her brother about her plans to run away. Form pairs and act out this scene, speaking the words and performing the actions that Konigsburg describes. What new things do you learn about the characters from actually seeing and hearing them talk together?

### Writer's Craft:  Prefixes

*"Indecent, not undecent," Claudia corrected.*

Both *in-* and *un-* are small words, **prefixes**, that come before words to mean "not." The word *indecent* means "not decent." As Claudia realizes, even though these two prefixes have the same meaning, they are not interchangeable.

The English language we speak today comes from the mixing of different, earlier languages. There are the short, blunt words of Anglo-Saxon from the early inhabitants of England; then the complicated, learned Latin of the Roman invaders; and later the medieval French of William the Conqueror. *In* is a Latin word for *not* and usually is combined with longer Latin words like *decent* and *convenient*. *Un* is the Anglo-Saxon negative and usually combines with short Old English words like *tidy* and *safe* and *sure*.

As you read, see which words use *in-* and which use *un-* as prefixes.

Literature Circle Guide for *From the Mixed-up Files of Mrs. Basil E. Frankweiler* • Scholastic Professional Books

Name _____  Date _____

## *From the Mixed-up Files of Mrs. Basil E. Frankweiler*
# Chapter 2

## Reading Strategy: Visualizing

E.L. Konigsburg has said that when she sits down to write she first has to get the "movie" rolling in her head. She has to visualize what she is going to describe. Good writers like Konigsburg provide us with enough details so that we too can imagine what they saw. As you read, notice what you are visualizing.

## Writing in Your Literature Response Journal

**A.** Write about one of these topics in your journal. Circle the topic you chose.

**1.** What does Claudia look like? What does her home look like? How does her little brother Kevin look? What does the train she and Jamie ride in look like?

**2.** What have you noticed about Claudia and Jamie's relationship? How do they treat each other? Why do you think this is so? Do they remind you of any other brothers and sisters you know, and if so, how? Does there seem to be anything special or unusual about their relationship? What makes for a good sibling relationship? What contributes to a difficult relationship?

**3.** Claudia seems to pay attention to everything, from the details of her plan to run away to how much lint is on the train seats. Try looking at the room around you as if you were she. What do you see that's different? What kind of details do *you* notice that you never noticed before?

**B.** What were your predictions, questions, observations, and connections as you read? Write about one of them in your journal. Check the response you chose.

❑ Prediction ❑ Question ❑ Observation ❑ Connection

**Name** _____ **Date** _____

## *From the Mixed-up Files of Mrs. Basil E. Frankweiler*
## Chapter 2

### For Your Discussion Group

✳ Make a list of all the questions you have about the book so far. Then divide them into two categories— questions that have a specific answer that you could find in the text ("How old is Jamie?") and interpretive questions that you could answer by inferring or drawing conclusions about what you've read ("Why is Claudia *really* running away?").

✳ Take turns sharing and answering your questions that have specific answers. As a team, you can probably clear up most of your factual confusions thus far about the book. You may have to decide that certain questions can't be answered just yet.

✳ Now share your interpretive questions. Choose one to discuss together. What are some possible answers? What other questions does this one make you think of?

### Writer's Craft:  Grammar Rules

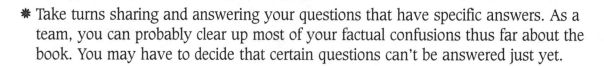

> "*Run* away *to? How can you run* away *and* to*? What kind of language is that?"* Claudia asked.
> "The American language," Jamie answered. "American James Kincaidian language."

Claudia is very concerned with speaking correctly, but sometimes she pays more attention to the rules of speech than to what is being said. In fact, even though it seems contradictory, Jamie can run *away* and *to*. Can you find other examples of words or phrases that seem to contradict one another but are actually correct?

Literature Circle Guide for *From the Mixed-up Files of Mrs. Basil E. Frankweiler* • Scholastic Professional Books

**Name** _____  **Date** _____

## *From the Mixed-up Files of Mrs. Basil E. Frankweiler*
## Chapter 3

### Reading Strategy: Making Connections

One way we make sense of new information is by connecting it
to what we already know or to experiences we've had. As you read, what other stories
or movies does this book remind you of? Are the characters or their adventures similar
to anything else you have read or seen? Once you have made a connection to another
story or movie, think about the similarities and differences.

### Writing in Your Literature Response Journal

**A.** Write about one of these topics in your journal. Circle the topic you chose.

**1.** Have you made a connection between this book and another book or movie? Explain what triggered this connection for you. What do you learn about *From the Mixed-up Files of Mrs. Basil E. Frankweiler* when you compare it to another story?

**2.** Alone in the large, quiet museum Claudia and Jamie curl up in an antique bed to go to sleep. Imagine yourself in a museum or historic home you've visited, long after closing time. (If you haven't been to one, imagine a department store, an amusement park, or a zoo.) Describe what you would do there, and what you would explore and see. Where would you sleep? How do you think it would feel to sleep there?

**3.** Mrs. Frankweiler is telling this story to her lawyer Saxonberg, and every now and then she puts in an aside, her own opinion about what is happening. What are you learning about Mrs. Frankweiler from these asides? Does anything she says surprise you? Explain why.

**B.** What were your predictions, questions, observations, and connections as you read? Write about one of them in your journal. Check the response you chose.

❏ Prediction    ❏ Question    ❏ Observation    ❏ Connection

Literature Circle Guide for *From the Mixed-up Files of Mrs. Basil E. Frankweiler* • Scholastic Professional Books

**Name** _____ **Date** _____

## *From the Mixed-up Files*
## *of Mrs. Basil E. Frankweiler*
## Chapter 3

### For Your Discussion Group

> *What happened was: they became a team, a family of two. There had been times before they ran away when they had acted like a team, but those were very different from feeling like a team.*

✳ How did Claudia and Jamie become a team? What does it mean to feel like a team? Have you ever felt like you were part of a team? Tell about that time. Compare your literature circle to a team.

### Writer's Craft: Specialized Vocabularies

> *Jamie . . . as chancellor of the exchequer, as holder of the veto power, and as tightwad of the year . . . got his wish.*

Every subject has its own special words. For instance, basketball has a **specialized vocabulary** to describe different shots and moves that someone who didn't know the game would have a hard time understanding. Jamie, the financial wizard, uses a specialized vocabulary about money. Knowing the meaning of specialized words a character uses can help you better understand that character. Make a list of these words and phrases from this chapter. Do you know what all the words mean? Divide the unfamiliar words among your group, and look them up in the dictionary.

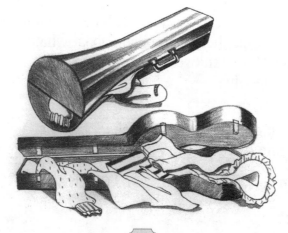

20

Literature Circle Guide for *From the Mixed-up Files of Mrs. Basil E. Frankweiler* • Scholastic Professional Books

**Name** _____ **Date** _____

*From the Mixed-up Files
of Mrs. Basil E. Frankweiler*

# Chapter 4

## Reading Strategy: Making Predictions

Up until now, the story has been about Claudia and Jamie's plans to run away. Now that they *have* run away, something else seems about to happen. What predictions can you make about what may happen? How is Mrs. Frankweiler going to become part of the story? What role will the angel sculpture play? Remember to revise your predictions as you continue to read—a skillful writer will always surprise you.

## Writing in Your Literature Response Journal

**A.** **Write about one of these topics in your journal. Circle the topic you chose.**

**1.** Look at the map of the Metropolitan Museum of Art, and imagine that Claudia has asked you to decide which exhibit to visit first. Which room would you choose and why?

**2.** *She took good long whiffs of the wonderful essence of detergent and clean dacron-cotton which floated down with the petticoat. Next to any kind of elegance, Claudia loved good clean smells.*

E.L. Konigsburg is wonderful at describing the sensations that her characters experience. As you read, you can feel the coldness of the museum's tiled bathroom, the silence of night, the discomfort of wearing too many layers of clothes.

Think about a time when you were very scared or very happy. Use all your senses to conjure up a picture in your mind of that time. What do you smell, hear, feel, and see? Write a description using as many sensory details as you can.

**B.** **What were your predictions, questions, observations, and connections as you read? Write about one of them in your journal. Check the response you chose.**

❑ Prediction        ❑ Question        ❑ Observation        ❑ Connection

Literature Circle Guide for *From the Mixed-up Files of Mrs. Basil E. Frankweiler* • Scholastic Professional Books

**Name** _____ **Date** _____

## From the Mixed-up Files
## of Mrs. Basil E. Frankweiler
# Chapter 4

## For Your Discussion Group

✳ Why do you think Claudia is so intrigued by
the angel sculpture? What does Mrs.
Frankweiler mean when she writes, *"The mystery only intrigued her; the magic trapped her."*
Remember this is an interpretive question—
there may be more that one right answer.

✳ Read the following quote from Mrs. Frankweiler about school field trips. Does she
describe a field trip accurately, or does she leave out anything?

> *Since I'm sure this group was typical of all the school groups that I've
> observed at the museum, I can tell you what they were doing.*

How do you normally behave on a field trip? How do the other students act?
Why do you think Claudia and Jamie seem to be enjoying the tour more than the
other kids?

## Writer's Craft: Similies

One of the ways E.L. Konigsburg brings this story to life is with **similes**, comparisons of
two very different things. The following simile appears in the book:

> *Their stomachs felt like tubes of toothpaste that had been all squeezed
> out. Giant economy-sized tubes.*

A simile usually begins with the word *like* or *as* and helps the reader feel more vividly
what is being described. In the passage above, Claudia and James weren't just hungry
but absolutely squeezed out, empty. What other kinds of comparisons do you notice
Konigsburg using to bring her story to life?

Literature Circle Guide for *From the Mixed-up Files of Mrs. Basil E. Frankweiler* • Scholastic Professional Books

**Name** _____   **Date** _____

*From the Mixed-up Files
of Mrs. Basil E. Frankweiler*

## Chapter 5

### Reading Strategy: Focusing on Important Details

> *She had neither pencil nor paper to make notes. And she knew she
> wouldn't have a lot of time to read. So she decided that she would simply
> remember everything, absolutely everything she read.*

Of course, Claudia finds this exhausting and impossible. Sometimes we think that good
readers remember everything they read. They don't. They remember what's important,
what's interesting, and/or what means something to them. Good readers also find it
helpful to write about what they read.

### Writing in Your Literature Response Journal

**A.** **Write about one of these topics in your journal. Circle the topic you chose.**

**1.** When you finish a chapter, write about what was most interesting or what caught
your attention. Don't try to write down everything that happened, just stay
focused on the details that are most vivid in your mind. As you write, ask yourself
why those details stood out for you, what made them so interesting.

**2.** Even though she has run away from home, Claudia has kept a lot of habits and
routines from her life in Greenwich. What kinds of routines does she stick to even
though she is living in a museum far from her parents? Why do you think she
does? What are some of your daily routines? Which ones would you like to run
away from? Which ones would you keep no matter what? Explain why.

**B.** **What were your predictions, questions, observations, and connections as you
read? Write about one of them in your journal. Check the response you chose.**

❏ Prediction     ❏ Question     ❏ Observation     ❏ Connection

Literature Circle Guide for *From the Mixed-up Files of Mrs. Basil E. Frankweiler* • Scholastic Professional Books

**Name** _____   **Date** _____

## *From the Mixed-up Files of Mrs. Basil E. Frankweiler*
## Chapter 5

### For Your Discussion Group

❋ Begin by having everyone in your group talk about a time when they were homesick. Describe that time and what made it so hard.

❋ Now think about Jamie and Claudia. At the end of Chapter 5, they begin to question why they are not homesick. Why do *they* think they do not miss their parents? Why do you think they don't? Should they miss their mother and father? Tell why or why not.

❋ Remember to respect everyone's opinion as you talk. Sometimes you may find yourself changing your mind. That's a positive sign of a powerful discussion.

### Writer's Craft:  Aphorisms

An **aphorism** is a short saying that captures some general truth about the way things are. E.L. Konigsburg uses the following aphorism in the book:

> *The only ways to get to know someone are to live with him or play cards with him.*

Often aphorisms are witty and catch you by surprise, just as Jamie does above when he talks about how to learn about someone. Mrs. Frankweiler, a woman of strong opinions, often speaks in aphorisms. For instance, in the first chapter she comments, "Flattery is as important a machine as the lever." What other aphorisms of hers do you notice? What do they mean? Do you agree or disagree with them?

Name _____   Date _____

## From the Mixed-up Files of Mrs. Basil E. Frankweiler
## Chapters 6–7

## Reading Strategy: Paying Attention to Inevitable Surprises

A skillful writer will constantly surprise us, yet the best surprises are those that seem inevitable: Once we look back, *of course* that was bound to happen, we tell ourselves. Pay attention to one of the surprises in these two chapters. What was startling about it? What was also inevitable?

## Writing in Your Literature Response Journal

**A.** Write about one of these topics in your journal. Circle the topic you chose.

**1.** Think about the inevitable surprises in this section. Look back earlier in the book, to see how Konigsburg subtly gave you clues about what was going to happen in these chapters.

**2.** By now we know that Claudia is an amazing planner and that Jamie is a money expert. If you had run away with Claudia and Jamie, what special skills would you have brought to the adventure? If you were with them, what would have been different? Write your own scene in the museum with Claudia and Jamie and you!

**3.** E.L. Konigsburg is an artist as well as a writer and did the illustrations for this book. What is your impression of the drawings? Which one did you look at the longest? Which ones have you gone back to? Have the pictures told you anything the text did not?

**B.** What were your predictions, questions, observations, and connections as you read? Write about one of them in your journal. Check the response you chose.

❏ Prediction     ❏ Question     ❏ Observation     ❏ Connection

**Name** _____ **Date** _____

## *From the Mixed-up Files of Mrs. Basil E. Frankweiler*
## Chapters 6–7

### For Your Discussion Group

✳ Before you begin to talk, take a moment and have everyone in the group pick out what they think is the most important sentence in these two chapters. Why is it the most important sentence?

✳ Now have everyone in the group share their sentences. Most will be different, but some may be the same, suggesting that there is some extra importance in these sentences. What is it?

✳ Talk together about why you chose the sentences you did. What is important to you about these chapters and this book? (Remember, a group discussion is richest when the members have different opinions and can share them openly.)

### Writer's Craft:  Semicolons

In the passage below, each of the clauses separated by a semicolon is complete or independent. Each clause can stand on its own as a sentence.

> *They weren't anxious to hear the talk about mummies again; they never watched repeats on television, either.*

In fact, if Konigsburg had used a period instead of a semicolon, it would have been absolutely correct punctuation. Why did she choose to use semicolons? When two sentences are part of the same idea, a writer can highlight the close relationship by using a semicolon instead of a period to separate them. The choice you make has a lot to do with your style as a writer. E.L. Konigsburg really likes to use semicolons. As you read, notice how she uses them to connect sentences and ideas.

Literature Circle Guide for *From the Mixed-up Files of Mrs. Basil E. Frankweiler* • Scholastic Professional Books

**Name** _____  **Date** _____

## From the Mixed-up Files
## of Mrs. Basil E. Frankweiler
# Chapter 8

## Reading Strategy: Noticing What's Left Out

Although Claudia seems to think of everything, is there anything you've noticed she doesn't ever mention or think about? What a character does *not* say or *not* do or *not* think can often be as revealing as actions. Make a list of everything you would have been thinking of or doing on this adventure that Claudia never even considers.

## Writing in Your Literature Response Journal

**A.** Write about one of these topics in your journal. Circle the topic you chose.

**1.** Look over the list you made about the things Claudia has not mentioned or done. What does your list tell you about her? What does it tell you about yourself?

**2.** During the course of their adventure, Jamie and Claudia are changing. Describe these changes. Are the changes positive or negative? Tell why. Have you ever had an experience that changed you? What was it? How did it affect you?

**3.** Jamie says that Claudia imagines herself being like Joan of Arc, Clara Barton, and Florence Nightingale. What about those women do you think is appealing to her? Who are your heroes and heroines? What qualities of theirs do you wish you had?

**B.** What were your predictions, questions, observations, and connections as you read? Write about one of them in your journal. Check the response you chose.

❑ Prediction     ❑ Question     ❑ Observation     ❑ Connection

Literature Circle Guide for *From the Mixed-up Files of Mrs. Basil E. Frankweiler* • Scholastic Professional Books

Name _____  Date _____

## *From the Mixed-up Files of Mrs. Basil E. Frankweiler*
## Chapter 8

### For Your Discussion Group

✴ As she indicates in the following passage, Claudia want to be different:

> *I want to be different when I go back. I, Claudia Kincaid, want to be different when I go back.*

✴ Why does she want to be different? Why isn't running away enough? Do you want to be different or more like your friends? What about most kids? What are some of the ways kids in your school try to be the same? What are some ways they try to be different?

### Writer's Craft: Adverbs and Adjectives

> *"I want to know how to go back to Greenwich different."*
> *Jamie shook his head. "If you want to go different, you take a subway to 125th Street and then take the train."*
> *"I didn't say* differently, *I said* different. *I want to go back different."*

Claudia's constant attention to grammar irritates her brother, but she realizes how confusing it can be if people don't know how to use words correctly. For instance, if her brother had known the difference between an adverb and adjective, he would never have misunderstood her. An **adverb** modifies or is connected to a verb while an **adjective** modifies a noun: *Claudia* wants to be different when she goes back; she doesn't want *to go* differently. As you listen to people around you talk, notice as Claudia does, if they are using adjectives and adverbs correctly.

Literature Circle Guide for *From the Mixed-up Files of Mrs. Basil E. Frankweiler* • Scholastic Professional Books

Name _____    Date _____

## From the Mixed-up Files
## of Mrs. Basil E. Frankweiler
# Chapters 9–10

## Reading Strategy: Rereading

That makes sense now! When you reach the end of a good book, suddenly the whole picture is clear and all the pieces fit together. A lot of times, readers find themselves wanting to look back at sections that had originally confused them to put everything into its proper place. Like many readers of this book, you may even want to go back and reread the whole thing!

## Writing in Your Literature Response Journal

**A.** Write about one of these topics in your journal. Circle the topic you chose.

**1.** Reread Mrs. Frankweiler's first letter or some of her asides. What do you notice now that you've finished reading the book?

**2.** What is Mrs. Frankweiler saying about learning in the passage below?

*I think you should learn, of course, and some days you must learn a great deal. But you should also have days when you allow what is already in you to swell up inside of you until it touches everything. And you can feel it inside of you. If you never take time out to let that happen, then you just accumulate facts, and they begin to rattle around inside of you. You can make noise with them, but never really feel anything with them. It's hollow.*

How can it "swell up inside of you?" What is the difference between accumulating facts and learning? What do you think Claudia has learned on her adventure? What have you learned from reading this book?

**B. What were your predictions, questions, observations, and connections as you read? Write about one of them in your journal. Check the response you chose.**

☐ Prediction    ☐ Question    ☐ Observation    ☐ Connection

Literature Circle Guide for *From the Mixed-up Files of Mrs. Basil E. Frankweiler* • Scholastic Professional Books

Name _____     Date _____

## From the Mixed-up Files
## of Mrs. Basil E. Frankweiler
# Chapters 9–10

### For Your Discussion Group

*Finding a secret can make
everything else unimportant.*

❋ Make a list of the secrets each of the
main characters—Mrs. Frankweiler,
Claudia, and Jamie—keeps. Which secret
do you think is the most important one,
and why? How do you feel about
secrets? Do you like to keep them? Explain why or why not.

❋ What do you think about the secret Claudia and Jamie get from Mrs. Frankweiler?
What if Mrs. Frankweiler hadn't had that piece of paper, or if Claudia and Jamie had
never found it? How would the ending of the story be different?

### Writer's Craft: Connotations and Denotations

*Claudia poked Jamie, "Never call people* dead; *it makes others feel bad.
Say 'deceased' or 'passed away.'"*

All three words or expressions—*dead, deceased, passed away*—mean exactly the same
thing, but they don't *feel* the same. *Dead* is a short, blunt word that feels final. *Deceased*
and *passed away* are softer and seem to suggest that someone has disappeared but not
forever. The **denotation** (or meaning) of the words is the same, but the **connotation**
(or feeling) of each word is different. Can you think of any other words that mean the
same but evoke different kinds of feelings?

*Literature Circle Guide for From the Mixed-up Files of Mrs. Basil E. Frankweiler* • Scholastic Professional Books

## *From the Mixed-up Files of Mrs. Basil E. Frankweiler*
# After Reading

The characters in *From the Mixed-up Files of Mrs. Basil E. Frankweiler* all have many opinions—about art, money, flattery, secrets—but what does the author, E.L. Konigsburg, think about these different issues?

One way we can begin to figure out what the author thinks is to look at what different characters say about an issue and the different things that happen to them. For instance, what does Mrs. Frankweiler say about secrets? What kinds of secrets does she keep? Do these secrets hurt the characters or help them?

✳ In order to help you begin to interpret some of the ideas in this book, choose one of the big issues below that is frequently mentioned in the book.

      secrets    money    learning    art    beauty    flattery

You can also choose any other important issue in the book.

✳ Now go back through the book and write down what all the different characters have to say about this issue. Then think about what the characters actually *do*. For instance, what does Mrs. Frankweiler actually do with her money? Next write down what happens to all the characters with regard to that particular issue. For example, you might observe that by the end of the story Jamie has lost all of this hard-won money. Finally record any scenes that you feel have something to do with this issue.

✳ What you now have before you are the facts, the evidence from the book of what was said and what happened. Looking it over, what do you think E.L. Konigsburg was trying to show the reader about the issues you are considering? Try to present your interpretation in a sentence or two. Talk about it with a member of your group. Have they interpreted the evidence differently, and if so, how?

Literature Circle Guide for *From the Mixed-up File of Mrs. Basil E. Frankweiler* • Scholastic Professional Books

# Individual Projects

**1.** Mrs. Frankweiler has a lot of opinions. Go back through the book and collect 10 to 20 of your favorite quotes or aphorisms from her. You can put them in a collection called "Wisdom from Mrs. Frankweiler." Include an explanation for each quote, telling why you selected it and why you think it's true.

**2.** Michelangelo lived into his eighties and never stopped sculpting. Find out more about his life and work so you can determine when he might have created the Angel. Which of his other works do you think it looks like? For instance, the *Madonna della Pietà* from Michelangelo's youth is very different than the Pietà he did as an old man. Present your findings to your group.

- - - - - - - - - - - - - - - - - - - - - - - - - - - - - - - - - - - - - - - - - - -

# Group Projects

**1.** Create your own classroom museum. You can use class artwork or copies of work from famous artists, or a combination. You may want to create a museum about American kids or a local natural history museum. Decide what the focus of your museum will be and its audience. Then decide what kinds of objects to include, how to arrange them, and what you might want to say or write about them. When you are done, arrange a time for your fellow classmates to visit your museum.

**2.** *From the Mixed-up Files of Mrs. Basil E. Frankweiler* won the Newbery Medal for 1967. This means that a group of people representing the Newbery Medal decided it was the very best book of that year. Imagine your literature circle is voting on a book award. Would you vote *From the Mixed-up Files of Mrs. Basil E. Frankweiler* as one of the best books you have read? Explain your reasoning. Create your own book award to give to books your group wants to recommend to other people. What will you call the award? What will the medal or certificate look like?

**3.** Claudia and Jamie do a lot of traveling—from Connecticut to New York by train, around New York City on foot and on buses, and through the museum itself. Have different group members draw maps for different parts of their journey. Obtain New York City street and bus maps from a guidebook in the library or on the Internet. Also, you can make a copy of the map of the Metropolitan Museum of Art in the book. With colored markers, draw Jamie and Claudia's routes on different days of their adventure.

Literature Circle Guide for *From the Mixed-up Files of Mrs. Basil E. Frankweiler* • Scholastic Professional Books